Arranged by Richard Harris

FLUTE PART

Contents

Title	Composer	page	track
Theme from *Star Wars*	John Williams	2	1
Theme from *James Bond*	Monty Norman	4	2
Circle of life with Nants' Ingonyama from *The Lion King*	Elton John/Tim Rice/Hans Zimmer/Lebo M.	6	3
Hedwig's theme and Mr Longbottom flies from *Harry Potter*	John Williams	8	4
Theme from *Chariots of Fire*	Vangelis	9	5
Theme from *Batman*	Danny Elfman	10	6
My heart will go on from *Titanic*	Will Jennings/James Horner	11	7
He's a pirate from *Pirates of the Caribbean*	Klaus Badelt/Hans Zimmer/Geoffrey Zanelli	12	8
Theme from *Superman*	John Williams	14	9
The ring goes south from *Lord of the Rings: The Fellowship of the Ring*	Howard Shore	16	10

Using the online backing tracks

The backing tracks are available to download from fabermusic.com/audio and a PDF of the piano accompaniment is available to download from the product page on fabermusic.com/shop.

© 2008 by Faber Music Ltd
First published in 2008 by Faber Music Ltd
Bloomsbury House
74–77 Great Russell Street
London WC1B 3DA
Music processed by Jackie Leigh
Cover design by Kenosha
Printed in England by Caligraving Ltd
All rights reserved

ISBN10: 0-571-52822-8
EAN13: 978-0-571-52822-6

Backing tracks created and engineered by Ned Bennett
Produced by Leigh Rumsey
℗ 2008 Faber Music Ltd © 2008 Faber Music Ltd

Theme from *Star Wars*

Music by John Williams

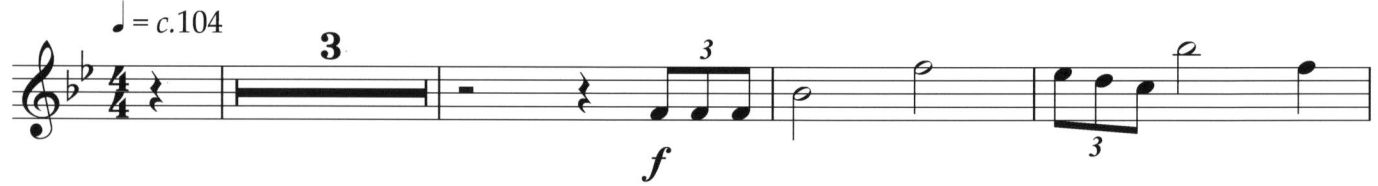

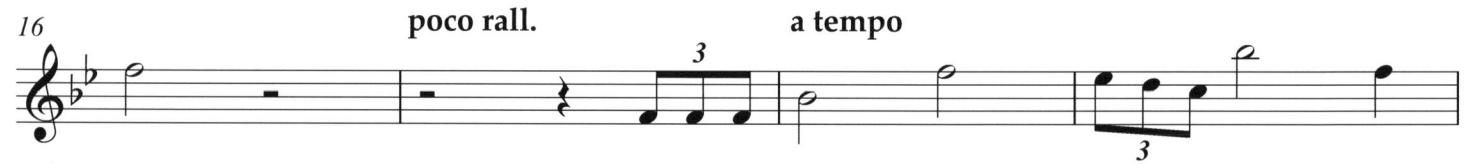
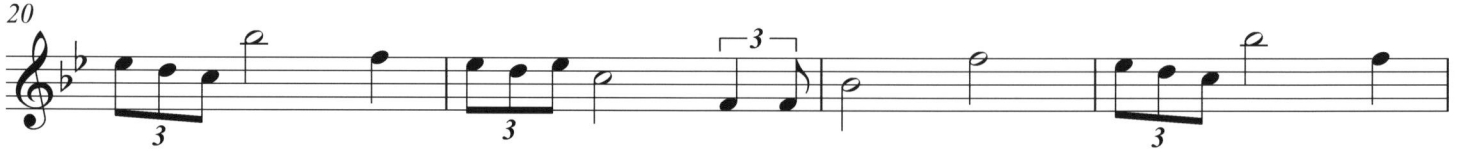
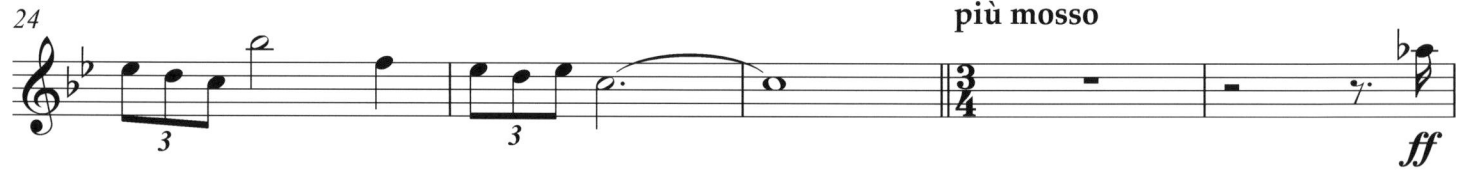

© 1977 Bantha Music, USA
Warner/Chappell North America Ltd, London W6 8BS

Theme from *James Bond*

Music by Monty Norman

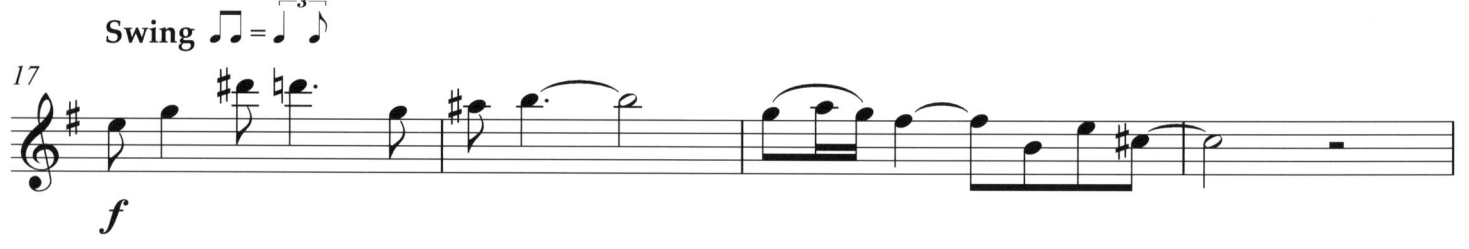

© 1962 EMI United Partnership Ltd, London WC2H 0QY (Publishing) and Alfred Publishing Co, USA (Print)
Administered in Europe by Faber Music Ltd

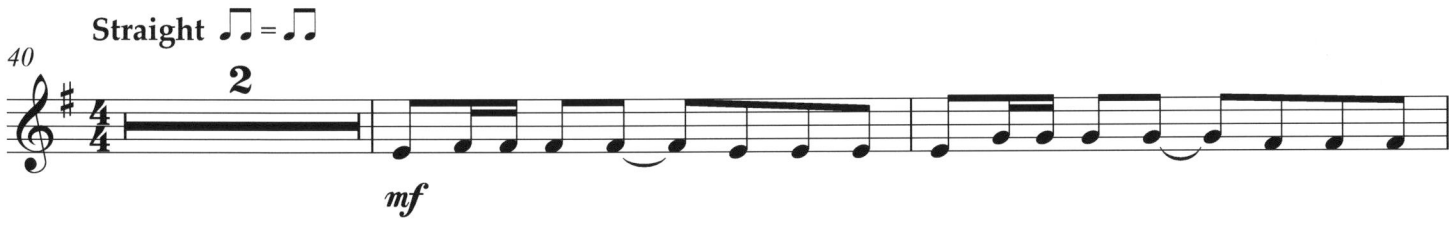

Circle of Life with Nants' Ingonyama
from *The Lion King*

Music by Elton John
Words by Tim Rice
'Nants' Ingonyama' by Hans Zimmer and Lebo M.

© 1994 Wonderland Music Co Inc, USA
Warner/Chappell Artemis Music Ltd, London W6 8BS

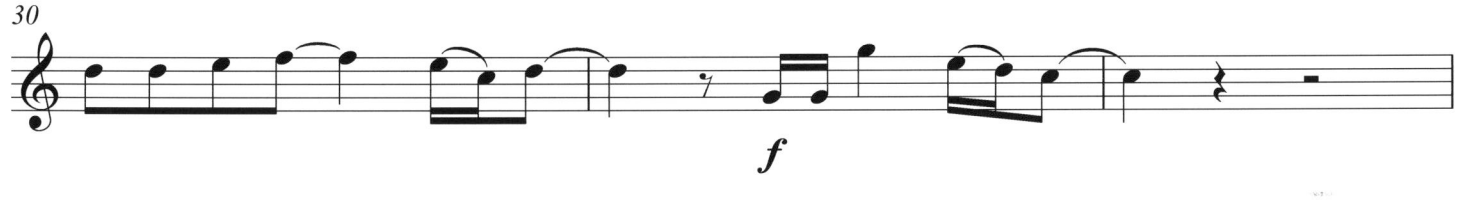
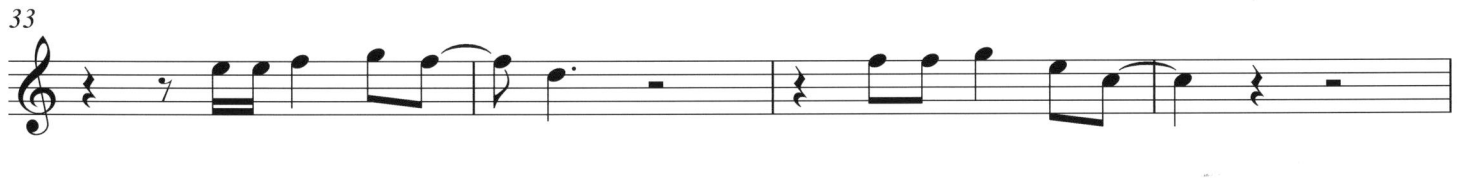

Hedwig's theme and Mr Longbottom flies
from *Harry Potter and the Philosopher's Stone*

Music by John Williams

Theme from *Chariots of Fire*

Music by Vangelis

Theme from *Batman*

Words and Music by Danny Elfman

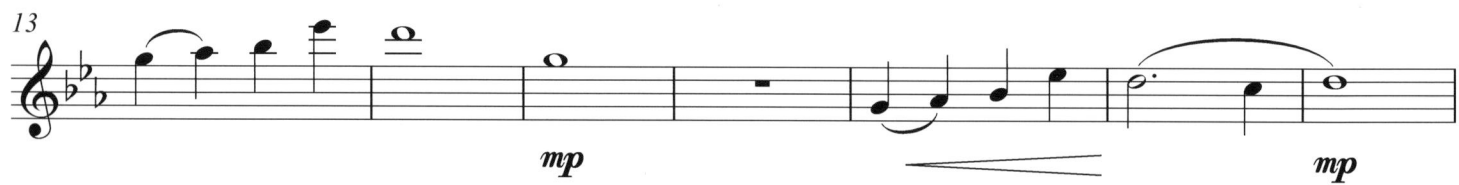

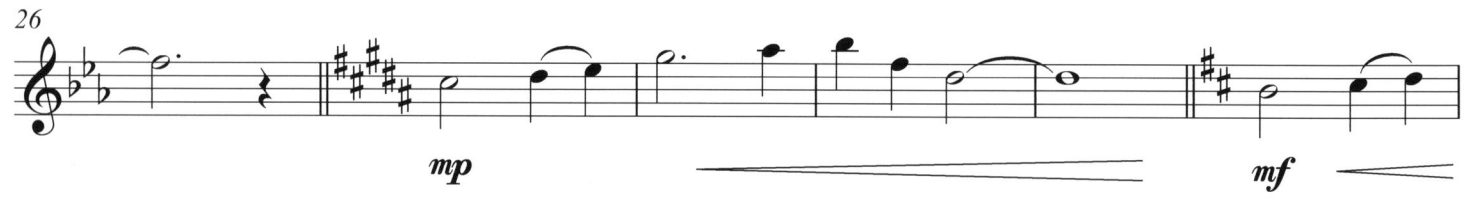
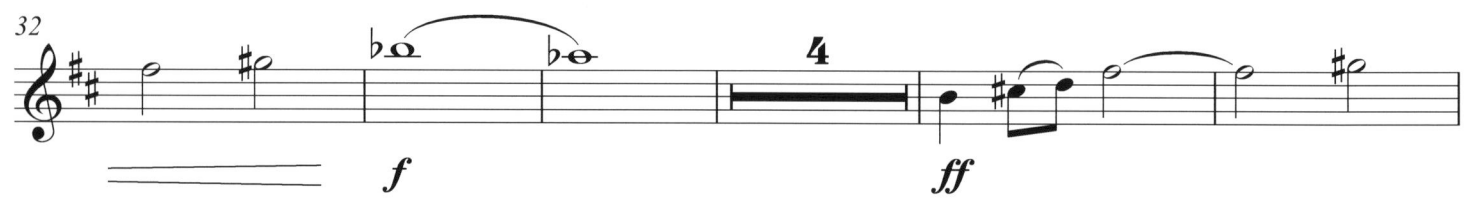
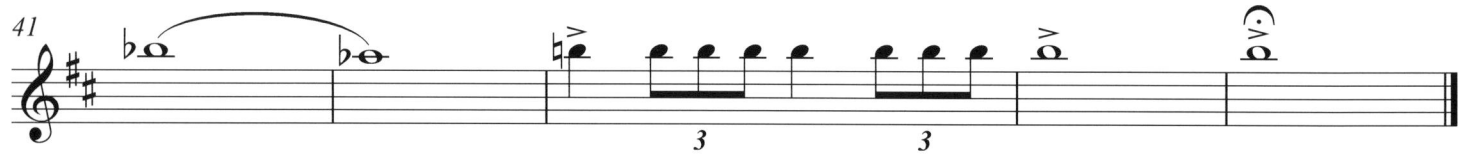

© 1989 Warner-Tamerlane Pub Corp, USA
Warner/Chappell North America Ltd, London W6 8BS

He's a pirate
from *Pirates of the Caribbean*

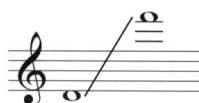

Words and Music by Klaus Badelt,
Hans Zimmer and Geoffrey Zanelli

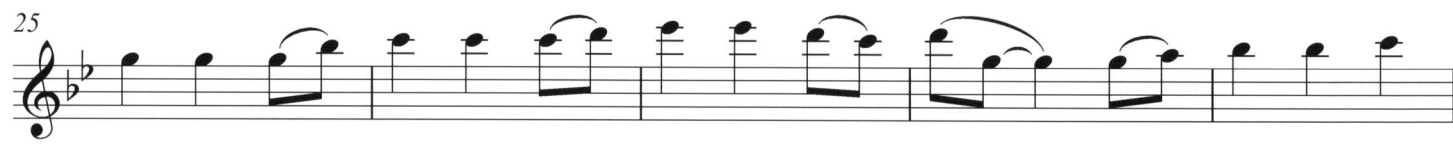
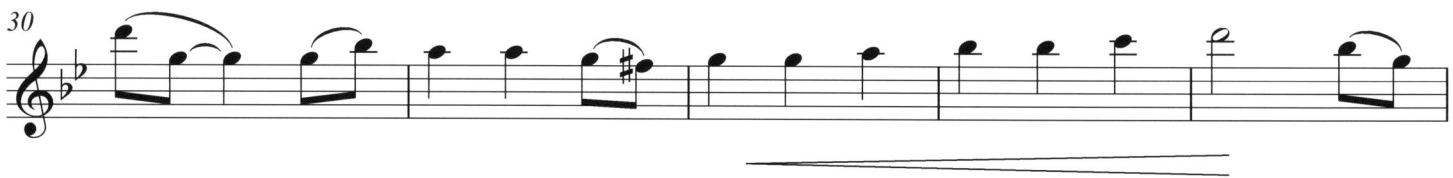

© 2003 Walt Disney Music (USA) Co, USA
Warner/Chappell Artemis Music Ltd, London W6 8BS

Theme from *Superman*

Music by John Williams

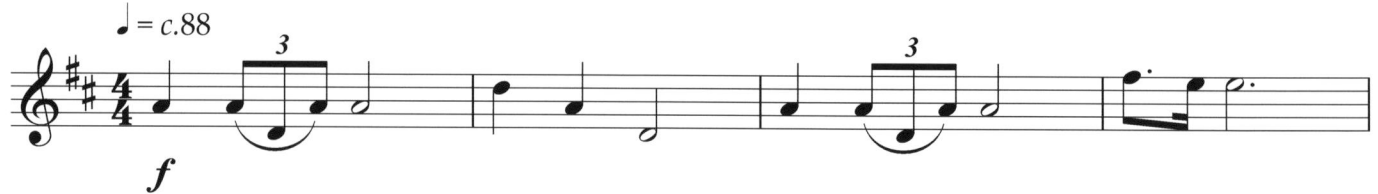

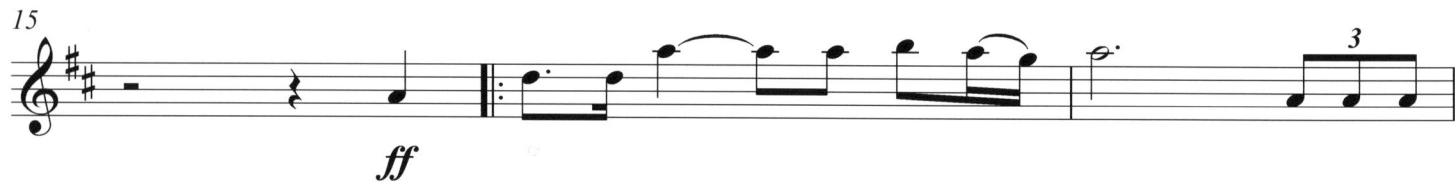

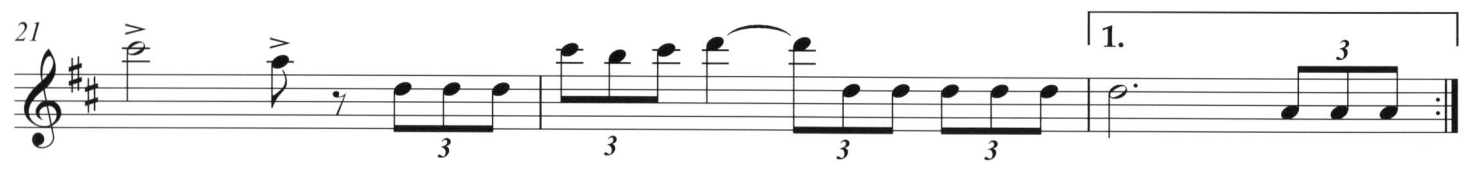
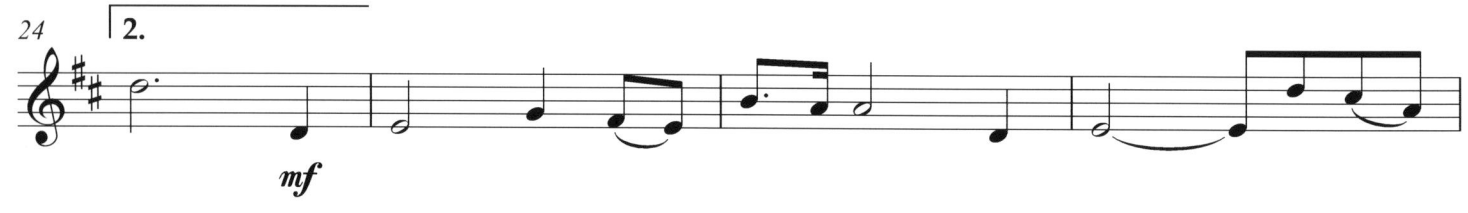

© 1978 Warner-Tamerlane Publishing Corp, USA
Warner/Chappell North America Ltd, London W6 8BS